Did pirates really make people walk the plank? What was life like on a pirate ship? Is there any buried treasure around today?

Dig up the answers to these questions and more in . . .

Magic Tree House®
Research Guide
PIRATES

A nonfiction companion to
Pirates Past Noon

It's Jack and Annie's very own guide to pirates!

Including:
- Pirate ships
- Pirate weapons
- Pirate treasure
- Real-life pirate stories

And much more!

Here's what people are saying about the Magic Tree House® Research Guides:

The Research Guide is like the other half of the story. The facts make the adventure even more amazing.—Louis S., age 10

My eight-year-old son completed <u>Knights and Castles</u> in record time and loved every minute of it.—Claire G., parent

The Research Guides are perfect complements to the Magic Tree House books. —Cecelia D., parent

These guides are all teachers need to introduce nonfiction and research.—Donna J., media specialist

With the Magic Tree House Research Guides and the companion fiction titles, teachers have the perfect combination for teaching reading skills across the curriculum.—Lee Ann D., media specialist

Magic Tree House®
Research Guide
PIRATES

A nonfiction companion to
Pirates Past Noon

by Will Osborne
and Mary Pope Osborne

illustrated by Sal Murdocca

A STEPPING STONE BOOK™
Random House 🏠 New York

www.randomhouse.com/magictreehouse

Library of Congress Cataloging-in-Publication Data
Osborne, Will.
Pirates / by Will Osborne and Mary Pope Osborne ;
illustrated by Sal Murdocca.   p.   cm. — (Magic tree house research guide)
"A nonfiction companion to Pirates past noon."
ISBN 0-375-80299-1 (trade) — ISBN 0-375-90299-6 (lib. bdg.)
1. Pirates—Juvenile literature.   I. Osborne, Mary Pope. Pirates past noon.
II. Murdocca, Sal.   III. Osborne, Mary Pope. Pirates past noon.   IV. Title.
V. Series.   G535 .O78 2001   910.4'5—dc21   00-062551

Printed in the United States of America   May 2001   10 9 8 7 6 5 4 3 2 1

Random House, Inc.   New York, Toronto, London, Sydney, Auckland

For Terry and Gina King

Historical Consultant:

DR. DAVID STARKEY, Department of History, University of Hull, Hull, United Kingdom.

Education Consultant:

MELINDA MURPHY, Media Specialist, Reed Elementary School, Cypress Fairbanks Independent School District, Houston, Texas.

We would also like to thank Paul Coughlin for his ongoing photographic contribution to the series; Donna Williams of the Pennsylvania Historical and Museum Commission for her assistance on board the U.S. brig *Niagara;* and, again, our wonderful, creative team at Random House: Joanne Yates, Diane Landolf, Cathy Goldsmith, Mallory Loehr, and, always and especially, our editor, Shana Corey.

PIRATES

Contents

Dear Readers,

Our adventure with Captain Bones in Pirates Past Noon was really exciting—and scary! We were very happy to get back home to Frog Creek. But once we were home, we started to wonder about a lot of things.

Why did people become pirates? What was it like to live on a sailing ship? Were there ever any women pirates? Is any pirate treasure still buried today?

We definitely didn't want to go back and ask Captain Bones! So we did research to find the answers.

We went to the library. We found books about pirates and sailing ships. We learned that there have been pirates for thousands

of years! Then we checked the Internet. We found pictures of pirate flags and stories about famous pirates throughout history. We took lots of notes and drew pictures of the ships and flags. We also found some cool videos that helped us learn even more.

In this book, we're going to share our research with you. So get your notebook, get your backpack, and get ready to sail away into the exciting world of pirates!

Jack

Annie

1

The First Pirates

For as long as there have been ships sailing the seas, there have been pirates.

Pirates are sea robbers. They attack ships on the water and towns along sea-coasts.

There are many pirate legends and stories. The most famous are about pirates who lived over two hundred years ago. The pirates in these tales lead exciting lives. They obey no laws. They find buried treasure. They sing songs about their daring deeds.

The truth is that most real-life pirates of long ago led miserable lives. They spent long, boring days on the water. They ate rotten food. They caught terrible diseases. Many died in sea battles and shipwrecks.

The word pirate comes from the Greek word peirates, which means "attacker."

Pirates were outlaws. They lived in fear of being caught and punished for their crimes. Most often, the punishment for being a pirate was death.

Still, thousands of people over the years chose to become pi-

Thousands of pirates were hanged for their crimes at sea.

14

rates. Searching for treasure, they jumped aboard ships and set out on the open seas.

Greek Pirates

Some of the first pirates we know about lived nearly 3,000 years ago. They robbed trading ships sailing along the coast of ancient Greece (see map on page 24).

Trading ships carry goods and passengers back and forth between countries.

These ancient Greek pirates hid on islands near the shore. When a trading ship passed by, they rowed out and surprised the sailors. The pirates stole the ship's goods. They might also kidnap the sailors and take over the ship.

A Greek myth tells about pirates who kidnap the god Dionysus (DY-uh-NY-sus). Dionysus is the god of wine and

A myth is a story or legend that usually features heroes or gods.

celebration. In the myth, Dionysus turns into a lion. The pirates jump into the sea. Dionysus changes them all into dolphins.

Roman Pirates

A <u>port</u> is a town or city where ships can load and unload their goods.

Pirates were also a problem in ancient Rome. Thousands of pirates attacked ships carrying goods to and from Roman ports. These pirates even had their own pirate nation. It was on the coast of what is now Turkey.

The great Roman leader Julius Caesar (SEE-zur) was captured by pirates when he was a young man. The pirates held Caesar prisoner for over a

Julius Caesar

month. They let him go only after his father sent them money.

After he was rescued, Caesar led a fleet of ships to find the pirates. When the pirates were caught, Caesar had them all killed.

A <u>fleet</u> is a group of ships with one commander.

In 67 B.C., a Roman general named Pompey (POM-pee) led a war against all the pirates of ancient Rome. The Roman navy attacked the pirates' ships at sea. The Roman army attacked the pirates' camps on land. Over 3,000 pirates were captured or killed.

Oh, wow! Pompey's son later became a pirate himself!

Pompey

Pompey became known as Pompey the Great.

17

Pirates from the North

Around 700 A.D., Viking pirates began attacking villages along the coasts of Europe.

The Vikings came from Norway, Sweden, and Denmark. The word *Viking* means "sea raider" in the Norse language.

The Vikings were good sailors and shipbuilders. Their ships were called *longboats*. Longboats were very fast. They usually had a single sail and many oars. There was often a dragon's head carved on the front.

When Vikings attacked a village, they raced off their longboats screaming and waving swords and battle axes. They robbed homes and churches. They stole treasure and took captives.

For 400 years, Vikings raided villages in western Europe, Russia, and the Middle East. In spite of their fierce ways, many Vikings settled in the lands they invaded. They built homes. They farmed the land and raised families.

The Middle Ages was the time between about 450 and 1500 A.D.

Corsair is the French word for "pirate."

The Barbary Corsairs

Another group of sea raiders who began attacking ships during the Middle Ages was the *Barbary corsairs* (BAR-buh-ree kor-SAIRZ).

The Barbary corsairs were seamen from the northern coast of Africa. They lived in countries called the *Barbary States*.

The Barbary corsairs were more interested in capturing people than in

Barbary corsair

stealing treasure. They held their captives prisoner until a ransom was paid. If no one paid the ransom, they sometimes sold their captives as slaves.

Pirates of the Far East

From earliest times, pirates also roamed the seas of the Far East. They raided ships and coastal towns of China, Japan, Borneo, and the Spice Islands.

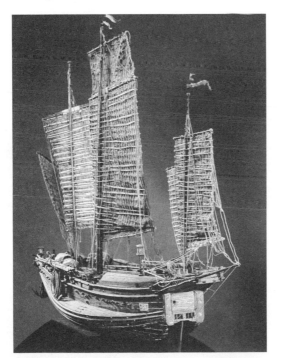

Chinese wooden sailing ships were called junks.

In the 1600s, a pirate named Cheng Chih-lung sailed the South China Sea with over 1,000 pirate ships. Later, a Chinese woman named Cheng I Sao led over 70,000 men and women sailors in pirate raids!

The ancient Chinese invented the <u>compass</u>, an instrument that helped sailors figure out where they were going.

Until the end of the 1400s, pirates mostly roamed the seas near Europe, Africa, and the Far East. But after 1492, pirates discovered a whole new world of ships to attack and rob.

Early Pirates

Greek pirates

Roman pirates

Vikings

Barbary corsairs

Asian pirates

Turn the page to see the world of early pirates.

This Way

North America

Atlantic Ocean

Africa

★ 1492 A.D.—
Columbus lands
on San Salvador
Island in Western
Hemisphere

South America

Time Line

Roman pirates

Greek pirates

1000 B.C.   800 B.C.   100 B.C.   400 A.D.

Europe

Mediterranean Sea

Asia

Pacific Ocean

Indian Ocean

Australia

all dates are approximate

Far East pirates			
Barbary corsairs			
Vikings			

| 700 A.D. | 1000 A.D. | 1500 A.D. | 2000 A.D. |

2

New World Pirates

In 1492, an explorer named Christopher Columbus made a sea voyage that changed the history of the world.

Columbus was hired by the king and queen of Spain. They wanted him to find a new way to get to the continent of Asia.

Columbus never found a new way to Asia. Instead, he landed on an island in the Caribbean (kar-uh-BEE-un) Sea.

The island was in a part of the world

A voyage (VOI-lj) is a long trip on a ship.

that people in Europe did not know about. It is the area we now call the *Western Hemisphere*. In Columbus's time, it became known as the *New World*.

The <u>Western Hemisphere</u> is the half of the earth that includes North, Central, and South America.

Native Americans lived here for thousands of years before Columbus.

After Columbus's voyage, Spanish explorers took over large areas of Central and South America. They destroyed the civilizations of the Native Americans. They stole their gold and silver. They stole their jewelry and precious stones.

The Spanish loaded their stolen goods onto treasure ships. These ships were great targets for pirates.

A <u>civilization</u> is a group of people with an advanced way of life that includes science, art, and, most often, writing.

Buccaneers

Some of the pirates who attacked Spanish treasure ships were called *buccaneers* (buk-uh-NEERZ).

Buccaneers were mostly outlaws from England, Holland, and France. In the 1600s, they settled on several islands in the Caribbean.

Buccaneers lived in camps. They hunted cattle and wild pigs on their islands. They learned from Native Americans how to cook meat on grills called *boucans* (BOO-kahnz). For this reason, they became known as "boucaniers," or "buccaneers."

Spain ruled the islands where the buccaneers lived. In the 1630s, Spanish rulers decided to drive them off the islands. The buccaneers were furious. They became pirates.

Buccaneers began attacking Spanish ships that sailed close to their islands. They would row out in canoes and attack a ship with guns, knives, and axes. Then they would steal the ship's treasure.

Privateers

A special kind of sea raider was called a *privateer* (pry-vuh-TEER). Privateers worked for a government. They had permission to attack ships that belonged to a country's enemies.

Privateers took treasure from the ships they attacked and kept it for themselves.

 The government papers that gave permission to privateers were called <u>letters of marque</u> (MARK).

Sometimes they gave part of their stolen treasure to the rulers who hired them.

In the 1600s, the rulers of many countries wanted a share of Spain's New World riches. They often hired privateers to attack Spanish ships and towns.

To their own countries, privateers were heroes. To their enemies, they were simply pirates.

How to Be a Buccaneer

Buccaneers were famous for their dirty, stinky ways. Here's how to become a buccaneer:

1. *Don't bathe or change clothes!*

Buccaneers didn't wash for months at a time. They made their clothes from animal skins and dressed in the same clothes every day—until they wore out!

2. *Don't wear shoes!*

Buccaneers almost always went bare-foot, even when they attacked a ship.

3. *Have a barbecue!*

Ships from all over the world stopped at the buccaneers' islands for hides, water, and supplies. The sailors often enjoyed the meat the buccaneers grilled on their boucans.

3

The Golden Age
of Pirates

The late 1600s and early 1700s are known
as *the Golden Age of Pirates.*

During the Golden Age, governments
hired more and more privateers to attack
enemy ships. Buccaneers robbed each
other, as well as the Spanish. The Barbary
corsairs continued to raid ships all over the
Mediterranean Sea. And as colonies were
established in North America, pirates of all

kinds attacked the ships that traded with them.

The seas became so dangerous that many countries began to crack down on piracy. They passed strict laws against pirates and anyone who traded with them. They sent warships to hunt pirates down.

Hundreds of pirates were killed in battle. Others were put on trial and hanged for their crimes.

In the 1720s, the Golden Age of Pirates came to an end. But by then, a handful of pirates had become timeless legends.

Jack and Annie's
Gallery
of
Pirates

Including tales and drawings
of the most famous pirates
of all time

Sir Francis Drake

Sir Francis Drake was an English explorer, privateer, and pirate. He was also the first Englishman to sail around the world.

When Drake was a young man, a ship he was on was attacked by the Spanish. Many of his friends were killed. For the rest of his life, Drake hated the Spanish.

In 1577, Drake began his voyage around the world. Along the way, he attacked many Spanish ships and towns. The voyage took three years. Drake returned with a ship filled with treasure.

Drake was knighted by Queen Elizabeth I. Privateers like Sir Francis Drake became known as the Sea Dogs of Queen Elizabeth. They were heroes in England. But the Spanish thought they were evil pirates.

Henry Morgan

Henry Morgan was a famous buccaneer. He lived on the island of Jamaica in the Caribbean.

Jamaica was ruled by England. In the 1660s, the Spanish tried to take over Jamaica. The governor of Jamaica gave Morgan and other buccaneers permission to attack Spanish ships and towns.

Morgan led many attacks against the

Spanish. He was known for his bravery—
and for his cruelty and wild ways. He attacked Spanish towns even after England
and Spain had stopped fighting.

To keep peace with Spain, the king of
England had Morgan arrested. But
Morgan was such a hero in England that he
was never put on trial. He was later
knighted and named deputy governor of
Jamaica!

Captain Kidd

William Kidd was a New York sea captain. In 1695, the king of England hired Captain Kidd to hunt down pirates who were attacking trading ships. Instead, Captain Kidd and his crew *became* pirates—and began attacking trading ships themselves!

When he returned from his voyage,

Captain Kidd was put on trial. He claimed his crew had forced him to become a pirate. But Kidd was found guilty and hanged in 1701.

Captain Kidd buried some of his treasure before he was caught. Later, many legends grew up about the hidden treasure of Captain Kidd.

Long Ben
(Henry Avery)

Henry "Long Ben" Avery started out as a sailor in the British navy. In 1694, he was hired as a privateer. When the crew of his privateer ship didn't receive any pay, they decided to become pirates. They elected Long Ben as their captain.

Long Ben and his crew captured a sailing ship from India. The ship was loaded with diamonds and other treasure. The treasure was worth over $400 million in today's money!

Long Ben retired with his great riches. But legend says he was later cheated out of all his money and died in poverty.

Black Bart (Bartholomew Roberts)

Bartholomew Roberts was the most successful pirate of the Golden Age. He began his pirate career as a regular sailor.

In 1719, a ship he was sailing on was at-

tacked by pirates. Roberts joined them and became a pirate himself. The pirates later made him captain of the ship. Roberts then became known as Black Bart.

In less than four years, Black Bart captured 400 ships! He was finally killed in a sea battle with the British Royal Navy.

Calico Jack (John Rackham), Anne Bonny, and Mary Read

John Rackham was captain of a pirate ship

in the Caribbean in the early 1700s. He was called Calico Jack because he liked to wear colorful clothes made from a kind of cloth called *calico*.

Anne Bonny met Calico Jack while he was ashore on the island where she lived. They fell in love. Anne dressed as a man and joined Calico Jack's pirate crew.

On one of his pirate attacks, Calico Jack captured a young sailor. The sailor wanted to join the pirate crew. The sailor turned out to be another woman dressed as a man! The woman's name was Mary Read.

Anne Bonny and Mary Read sailed with Calico Jack until his ship was captured in 1720. Reports say only Anne and Mary fought to defend their pirate ship! All the men hid below deck. Calico Jack was hanged for his crimes. Anne Bonny and Mary Read were sent to prison.

52

Blackbeard
(Edward Teach)

Blackbeard was the most famous pirate of all time. But Blackbeard was a pirate for only two years, from 1716 to 1718!

Blackbeard got his nickname from his long, bushy black beard. When he went into battle, he would braid pieces of rope into his beard and long hair. Then he would set them on fire!

People were so afraid of Blackbeard that they almost always gave up without a fight. Finally, the governor of Virginia sent the navy to hunt Blackbeard down. The pirate fought like a wild man. He was finally killed by the crew of a navy ship.

Greek galley

4

Pirate Ships

Over the centuries, pirates have roamed the seas in many different kinds of ships.

Most early pirate ships were galleys. A galley is a big rowboat with sails. When there was a good wind, a galley's sails were used for extra speed.

The Barbary corsairs had huge galleys. It took nearly a hundred men to row them. They also carried troops of soldiers. These ships almost never went on long ocean voyages. There were so many men, there was hardly any room for supplies!

Barbary corsairs' galley

Sailing Ships

During the Golden Age of Pirates, most pirate ships were sailing ships. They used the wind to carry them on their long voyages in search of treasure.

These sailing ships were alike in many ways. They were all made of wood. They all had large sails made of heavy cloth. The sails hung from beams called *yardarms*. The yardarms were attached to tall poles called *masts*.

Pirate sailing ships all had space for storing supplies and treasure. Most carried several cannons and smaller guns for attacking other ships at sea.

A **cannon** is a large gun, usually mounted on wheels.

Pirate Ships

Made of wood

Large sails

Yardarms

Masts

Storage space

Guns

Kinds of Sailing Ships

There are many different kinds of sailing ships.

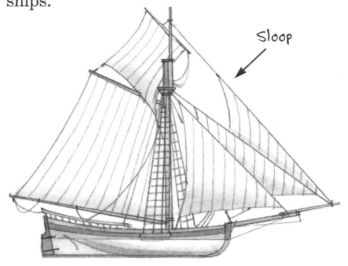

Sloop

Sloops were a favorite kind of ship for pirates. They are small ships with only one mast. Pirate sloops couldn't hold as many guns or men as larger ships. But in battle, they could move around more easily. Best of all, sloops were very fast.

Speed was important to pirates. Their ships had to be fast to catch ships they wanted to attack. They also had to be fast to escape from ships attacking *them*!

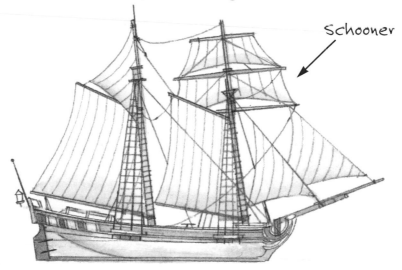

Schooner

Schooners (SKOO-nurz) and *brigantines* (BRIG-un-teenz) have two masts. They are also very fast. Schooners were popular with American privateers in the late 1700s and early 1800s.

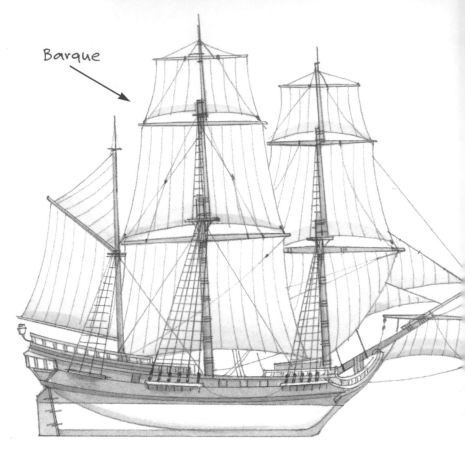

Barque

Barques (BARKS) have three or more masts. They are slower than smaller sailing ships. Some pirates liked barques because they could carry more guns—and more *treasure!*

Kinds of Sailing Ships

Sloops—one mast

Schooners—two masts

Brigantines—two masts

Barques— three or more masts

Turn the page to see the parts of a pirate ship.

This Way

Mast

Yardarm

Rudder

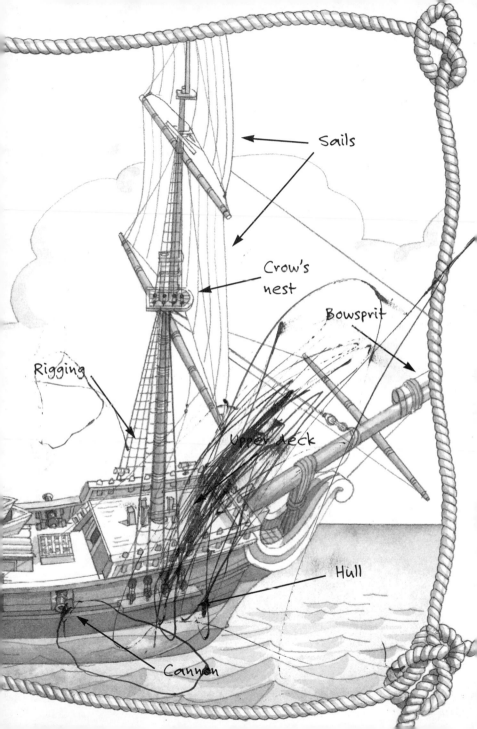

Sails

Crow's nest

Bowsprit

Rigging

Upper deck

Hull

Cannon

5

A Pirate's Life

Pirates were thieves, murderers, and kidnappers. They didn't obey the laws of any land. They did, however, obey rules on board their ships.

Pirates called their rules *the Articles*. The Articles told the men how to behave on board. They listed punishments for breaking the rules. They explained how stolen treasure would be shared by the crew and captain.

Every pirate ship had its own set of Articles. Here are some common rules:

Pirate Rules

1. Every man in the crew shall get an equal share of what is stolen.
2. No fighting.
3. No gambling.
4. No women allowed on board ship.
5. Weapons must be kept clean and ready.
6. Punishment for stealing, running away from a fight, or keeping secrets is DEATH!

Pirate Captains

There were many jobs on a pirate ship. The most important job was that of the captain.

The captain led the crew in battle. He also *navigated* the ship. This means he was in charge of getting the ship where it was supposed to go.

A pirate captain had to follow the Articles, too. If he didn't do a good job, the crew might throw him overboard and elect a new captain!

Even if the captain did a good job, the crew still had lots of power. They voted to decide where the ship would travel. They voted on where and when to go ashore. They voted on whether or not to attack a ship they met at sea.

The Quartermaster

The ship's *quartermaster* also had an important job.

The quartermaster decided what to steal from a captured ship. He divided up what the pirates stole. He handed out the food. And he told each man what work to do on board the ship.

Life at Sea

Pirate crews had to work hard to keep their ships in good shape. Sails and ropes had to be mended. Cannons had to be cleaned. Decks had to be washed.

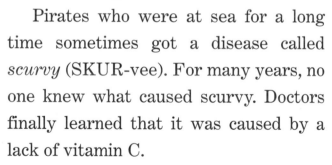

Hardtack

Food was hard to find on long sea voyages. Sometimes pirates took a few chickens on board for eggs. They also took dried meat and stale biscuits. The biscuits were called *hardtack*. Stories say pirates ate them in the dark so they wouldn't see the bugs inside!

British sailors were nicknamed limeys because they ate limes to prevent scurvy!

Pirates who were at sea for a long time sometimes got a disease called *scurvy* (SKUR-vee). For many years, no one knew what caused scurvy. Doctors finally learned that it was caused by a lack of vitamin C.

Fresh drinking water was hard to come by on long voyages. Pirates could not drink water from the salty sea. So their ships carried barrels of beer and bottles of wine and rum.

Long voyages often meant many days with little to do. Life on board ship could get boring. To pass the time, pirates gambled with dice. They sometimes fought with one another.

The Articles often had rules against gambling and fighting. It was the quartermaster's job to hand out punishments to anyone who broke the rules.

Yikes! There were lots of rats on pirate ships. They ate everything— even the wood of the ship!

Pirate Punishments

In some stories about pirates, a person who broke the rules was made to *walk the plank*. The person was blindfolded. His hands were tied. A wide plank was put over the ship's side. The person

71

walked to the end of the plank. Then he fell into the sea.

There is not much proof though, that walking the plank actually happened in real life. Pirates who broke the rules were much more likely to be whipped or shot.

Another terrible punishment was called *marooning* (muh-ROON-ing). People who were marooned were taken to a deserted island. They were put off the ship. The ship then sailed away, leaving the person alone.

The deserted island was usually tiny. The marooned person would starve to death, drown, or die of thirst. He was often left with a gun so he could take his own life.

Jack and Annie Present: Talk Like a Pirate

Show a leg, lubber! Or I'll send you to Davy Jones's locker!

Shiver me timbers, matey!

Show a leg!—Get up!

Pirates slept in hammocks. When they started to get out of a hammock, they would *show a leg* over the side.

Lubber—clumsy sailor

Lubber is short for *landlubber*—a person who is happier on land than at sea.

Davy Jones's locker—the bottom of the ocean

In the 1630s, a pirate named David Jones decided to sink a ship that he and his crew had attacked. After that, pirates said that anything sunk or thrown overboard (including people!) was *sent to Davy Jones's locker.*

Shiver me timbers!—Oh, wow!

Pirates called a ship's masts *timbers.* The timbers would *shiver,* or shake, in a storm.

Matey—friend

Sailors from the same ship are called shipmates. *Matey* is short for *shipmate.*

6

Pirate Treasure

Why were pirates willing to put up with terrible living conditions at sea? Why were they willing to be so mean and cruel? Why were they willing to risk dying for their crimes?

For most pirates, the answer was simple: *money*.

One successful raid on a treasure ship could make all the members of a pirate crew rich for the rest of their lives.

Booty is anything of value taken by force from an enemy.

Booty

Pirates called their stolen treasure *booty*. For pirates, the best booty was gold.

Gold was prized all over the world. Pirates dreamed of capturing ships full of gold coins, gold bars, or gold jewelry.

Spanish gold coins were called <u>doubloons</u> (duh-BLOONZ). Eight doubloons were worth a whole year's pay for a regular sailor!

Silver was also very valuable booty. Silver coins were called *pieces of eight.* That's because each coin was worth eight Spanish *reales* (ray-AH-layz)—about twenty-three dollars today.

Unfortunately for pirates, very few trading ships carried treasure chests filled with gold and silver. So the pirates usually had to settle for other booty.

Pieces
of eight

When pirates captured a ship, they took almost anything of value. They stole tobacco, spices, and sugar to sell when they reached land. They stole jewelry from the passengers. They stole guns, swords, and daggers from the crew.

Pirates also stole sails and ropes to use on their own ship. They stole food, water, beer, and wine to share among themselves. They stole any medicine they could find, too. Medicine was thought to be great booty because pirates suffered so much disease.

A ship
doctor's
medicine
chest

Blackbeard's famous pirate ship, the Queen Anne's Revenge, was once a French trading ship.

Sometimes pirates even stole the whole ship! They turned it into a pirate ship and forced the crew to join them. The choice they gave the crew was simple: *Join us or die!*

Pirate Booty

Gold doubloons

Silver pieces of eight

Tobacco, spices, and sugar

Jewelry

Guns, swords, and daggers

Sails and ropes

Food and water

Beer and wine

Medicine

Whole ship

Sharing the Booty

The Articles for a ship had strict rules about how booty was to be shared. Most members of the crew got an equal part of everything that was stolen. The captain, quartermaster, and ship's doctor usually got a little more than everyone else.

The punishment for anyone who tried to keep more than his share of the booty was death or marooning.

Buried Treasure

There are many stories about pirates burying chests full of booty on secret islands. The pirates in the stories often make maps showing where the treasure is buried.

Captain Kidd
burying
treasure

The truth is that pirates hardly ever buried their treasure. In real life, they usually divided the booty soon after it was stolen. Then each man spent most of his share as soon as he was on land again.

Sunken Treasure

There may not be any pirate treasure still buried on secret islands. But there is definitely pirate treasure at the bottom of the ocean.

Over the years, many pirate ships sank in storms. Others went down in battle. When a pirate ship sank, its treasure sank with it!

For centuries, people have searched for sunken pirate ships. None were ever found—until undersea divers recently made two amazing discoveries.

The *Whydah*

In 1984, a sea explorer named Barry Clifford found items from the wreck of the pirate ship *Whydah* (WID-uh). The *Whydah* was sunk off the coast of Massachusetts in 1717. It had belonged to a pirate called Black Sam Bellamy. The *Whydah* was filled with gold and silver coins.

These coins are from the wreck of the Whydah.

The *Queen Anne's Revenge*

In 1996, a research team discovered another sunken ship. This one was off the coast of North Carolina. The research team is now almost sure it is Blackbeard's ship, the *Queen Anne's Revenge*!

This bronze bell is thought to be from the <u>Queen Anne's Revenge</u>.

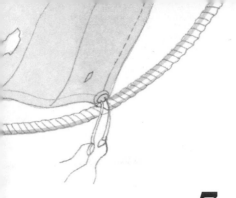

7

Pirate Attack!

Pirates used many weapons when they attacked another ship. Their best weapon
was often not a gun, a knife, or a sword. It
was surprise!

Sometimes pirates tried to fool the crew
of the ship they wanted to attack. They
pretended their pirate ship was an ordinary
trading ship. They hid their weapons. They
flew the flag of the other ship's country.

Some pirates even wore dresses and bonnets to fool the other ship's crew!

When their ship was next to the other ship, the pirates fired their cannons and raised their pirate flag. They threw *grappling irons* into the rigging of the other ship. They pulled on the ropes attached to the grappling irons and drew the ships together.

Grappling irons

The pirates jumped onto the deck of the other ship. They screamed and yelled. They fired pistols. They waved swords and daggers.

Pirates tried to be as scary as possible in an attack. They wanted their victims to surrender without a fight. Usually, that's exactly what happened! Most sailors were paid very poorly. They were not willing to give their lives to defend their ship's treasure.

Pirate Weapons

When they did fight, pirates used many different kinds of weapons.

Cutlass

The cutlass (KUT-lus) was the favorite weapon of pirates during the Golden Age. A cutlass was a short sword

90

with a wide, sharp blade. It had a hand guard to protect the pirate's fingers.

A cutlass was better than a long sword for fighting in a ship's tight spaces. It was also less likely to get tangled in the ship's rigging.

Pirates often fought with small knives called *daggers* (DAG-gurz). Like cutlasses, daggers were good for fighting in tight spaces.

Pirates liked daggers because they were easy to hide!

During the 1700s, many pirates carried pistols called *flintlocks* (FLINT-loks). Flintlock pistols could fire only one shot before reloading. So a pirate attacking a ship often carried a flintlock pistol in each hand.

Yikes!
After he fired its one shot, a pirate often used his flintlock pistol's handle as a club.

Pirates also had long guns called *muskets*. A musket's aim was more accurate than a flintlock pistol's. With a musket, a pirate could hit a target from 300 feet away.

Musket

Pirates sometimes began an attack by firing a musket at the other ship's *helmsman* (HELMZ-mun). The helmsman was the man steering the ship. If he was hit, the ship was much easier to capture.

Pirates used axes to cut through the rigging of the ship they were attacking.

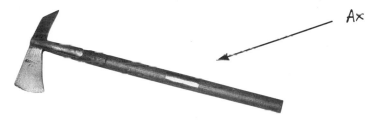

Ax

Without rigging, the sails would fall down—and the ship would be "dead in the water."

Pirates also used axes to smash down cabin doors and break open treasure chests.

Smoke bombs were sometimes used in

pirate attacks. Pirates made smoke bombs by filling a pot or a bottle with tar and rags. They would set the smoke bombs on fire. Then they would throw them onto the ship they were attacking. The thick black smoke added to the confusion and fear.

Pirates might also fire cannons in an attack. Cannonballs were made of stone or iron. They could easily rip through sails or smash the wood of a ship.

Pirates' Weapons

Cutlasses

Daggers

Flintlock pistols

Muskets

Axes

Smoke bombs

Cannons

Cannon

It took several men to load
and fire a cannon like this one.

Cannons were also used by other
ships *against* pirates. At the end of the
Golden Age, the British navy attacked
pirates with ships called *men-of-war*.

Men-of-war were huge. They could carry many more cannons than a pirate ship could carry. They hunted down pirates in seas throughout the world.

This is a model of the British man-of-war that attacked and defeated Black Bart.

Pirate Flags

A pirate flag was called a *Jolly Roger*. The first pirate flags were bright red. The name *Jolly Roger* may have come from the French words *joli rouge* (zho-LEE ROOZH), which mean "pretty red."

Here are some famous Jolly Rogers:

The Flag of Calico Jack

A skull, a skeleton, bones, or swords on a flag stood for violence and death.

The Flag of Blackbeard

The hourglass in the skeleton's hand meant time was running out for Blackbeard's victims!

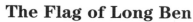

The Flag of Black Bart

On his flag, Black Bart dances with death!

The Flag of Long Ben

The skull on Long Ben's flag wears a bandanna—like Long Ben might have worn himself.

British sailors battling the Barbary corsairs.

8

Piracy After the Golden Age

The sea battles at the end of the Golden Age did not completely rid the world of pirates.

Barbary corsairs continued to attack ships near the Barbary Coast. Asian pirates still sailed the South China Sea. American privateers attacked British ships during the Revolutionary War.

In the 1800s, though, several events nearly wiped out piracy completely.

In 1816, the home port of the Barbary corsairs was destroyed. In 1849, the British navy destroyed a huge Asian pirate fleet. In 1856, many countries signed an agreement promising they would no longer hire privateers.

By then, the navies of many countries had begun to use steamships. Steamships didn't depend on the wind to move quickly across the sea. Pirates in their small sailing vessels were no match for the big, heavily armed steamships.

Steamships had engines that used steam power to turn big paddle wheels.

Pirates lived on, though, in adventure stories and legends.

Long John Silver was a ship's cook who became a pirate captain in _Treasure Island._

Treasure Island is the most famous pirate adventure story of all time. It tells the tale of a boy who battles with pirates while searching for hidden treasure. _Treasure Island_ was written in 1883 by Robert Louis Stevenson.

Peter Pan was written in 1904 by J. M. Barrie as a play for children. Millions of people now know Peter Pan through books, plays, and movies.

In <u>Peter Pan</u>, Peter battles the evil make-believe pirate Captain Hook.

Even today, there are new books and movies about pirates almost every year.

Pirates no longer capture chests full of pieces of eight and gold doubloons. They capture our imaginations instead.

Doing More Research

There's a lot more you can learn about real-life pirates.

The fun of research is seeing how many different sources you can explore.

Books

Most libraries and bookstores have books about pirates.

Here are some things to remember when you're using books for research:

1. You don't have to read the whole book. Check the table of contents and the index to find the topics you're interested in.

2. Write down the name of the book.

When you take notes, make sure you write down the name of the book in your notebook so you can find it again.

3. Never copy exactly from a book.

When you learn something new from a book, put it in your own words.

4. Make sure the book is nonfiction.

There are many books that tell make-believe stories about pirates and their adventures. Make-believe stories are called *fiction*. They're fun to read, but they're not good for research.

Research books have real facts and tell true stories. They are called *nonfiction*. A librarian or teacher can help you make sure the books you use for research are nonfiction.

Here are some good nonfiction books that tell the facts about pirates.

- *Bloodthirsty Pirates* by Richard Mead

- *Pirates* by Dina Anastasio

- *Pirates* (Fact or Fiction series) by Stewart Ross

- *Pirates!* by David Spence

- *Pirates* by Philip Steele

Museums

Museums that specialize in ships and sea travel are called *maritime* museums. These museums usually have exhibits of model ships, plus many of the things used by sailors through the centuries, like compasses and telescopes. Some even have ships that you can go aboard!

When you go to a maritime museum:
1. Be sure to take your notebook!
Write down anything you see that catches your interest. Draw pictures, too!

2. Ask questions.
There are almost always people at a museum who can help you find what you're looking for.

3. Check the museum calendar.

Many museums have special events and activities just for kids!

Ask your parents or teacher if there is a maritime museum near you. Here are some maritime museums around the country:

- Los Angeles Maritime Museum
  San Pedro, California

- The Mariners' Museum
  Newport News, Virginia

- Mystic Seaport
  Mystic, Connecticut

- North Carolina Maritime Museum
  Beaufort, North Carolina

- South Street Seaport Museum
  New York, New York

- Texas Maritime Museum
  Rockport, Texas

- U.S. Brig *Niagara*/Erie Maritime
  Museum
  Erie, Pennsylvania

Videos

Most movies about pirates are *fiction*. There are some videos, though, that tell the real story of pirates and how they lived.

There are also videos about explorers like Sir Francis Drake and about sailing ships and life at sea.

Check your library or video store for these and other nonfiction videos:

- *The Golden Age of Pirates and Buccaneers*
  from Tom James Productions

- *Pirates!*
  from the Discovery Channel

The Internet

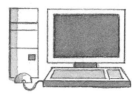

Many Internet Web sites have facts about pirates. Some even have games that help you learn more about pirates and the history of sailing ships.

Ask your teacher or your parents to help you find more Web sites like these:

- ils.unc.edu/maritime/home
- www.discovery.com/stories/history/pirates/pirates.html
- www.nationalgeographic.com/features/97/pirates
- www.nationalgeographic.com/silverbank
- www.piratesinfo.com
- www.ukoln.ac.uk/services/treasure

Good luck!

Index

27, 28, 29
cutlasses, 90–91, 94

daggers, 89, 91, 94
Dionysus, 15–16
doubloons, 78, 81,
    105
Drake, Sir Francis,
    41

Elizabeth I, 41

flintlocks, 91–92, 94

galleys, 55–56
Golden Age of
    Pirates, *see*
    pirates, Golden
    Age of
grappling irons, 88

hardtack, 70
helmsman, 93

Hook, Captain, 104

Jolly Rogers, 98–99
Jones, David, 75
junks, 21

Kidd, William,
    44–45, 82

letters of marque,
    32
Long Ben, *see*
    Avery, Henry
longboats, 18–19

marooning, 73, 82
men-of-war, 95–96,
    97
Middle Ages, 20
Morgan, Henry,
    42–43
muskets, 92, 93, 94

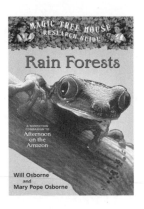

If you liked *Afternoon on the Amazon,*
you'll love finding out the facts
behind the fiction in

Magic Tree House® Research Guide

RAIN FORESTS

A nonfiction companion to
Afternoon on the Amazon

It's Jack and Annie's very
own guide to rain forests!

Look for it September 2001!

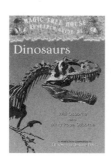
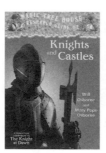
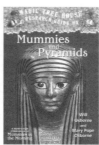

Other books by Mary Pope Osborne and Will Osborne:

Picture books:
Kate and the Beanstalk by Mary Pope Osborne
Mo and His Friends by Mary Pope Osborne
Moonhorse by Mary Pope Osborne
Rocking Horse Christmas by Mary Pope Osborne

First chapter books:
The *Magic Tree House®* series by Mary Pope Osborne

For middle-grade readers:
Adaline Falling Star by Mary Pope Osborne
American Tall Tales by Mary Pope Osborne
The Deadly Power of Medusa by Mary Pope Osborne
    and Will Osborne
Favorite Greek Myths by Mary Pope Osborne
Favorite Medieval Tales by Mary Pope Osborne
Favorite Norse Myths by Mary Pope Osborne
Jason and the Argonauts by Mary Pope Osborne
    and Will Osborne
Joe Magarac by Will Osborne
The Life of Jesus in Masterpieces of Art
    by Mary Pope Osborne

Mermaid Tales from Around the World

by Mary Pope Osborne

My Brother's Keeper by Mary Pope Osborne

My Secret War by Mary Pope Osborne

One World, Many Religions by Mary Pope Osborne

Spider Kane and the Mystery Under the May-Apple

(#1) by Mary Pope Osborne

Spider Kane and the Mystery at Jumbo Nightcrawler's

(#2) by Mary Pope Osborne

Standing in the Light by Mary Pope Osborne

13 Ghosts: Strange but True Stories by Will Osborne

For young-adult readers:

Haunted Waters by Mary Pope Osborne

Magic Tree House® Books

A STEPPING STONE BOOK™

Great authors write great books . . .
for fantastic first reading experiences!

Grades 1–3

Duz Shedd series
by Marjorie Weinman Sharmat
Junie B. Jones series by Barbara Park
Magic Tree House® series
by Mary Pope Osborne
Marvin Redpost series by Louis Sachar

Clyde Robert Bulla
The Chalk Box Kid
The Paint Brush Kid
White Bird

Jackie French Koller
Mole and Shrew All Year Through
Mole and Shrew Are Two
Mole and Shrew Have Jobs to Do

Jerry Spinelli
Tooter Pepperday
Blue Ribbon Blues: A Tooter Tale

Grades 2–4

A to Z Mysteries® series by Ron Roy
The Katie Lynn Cookie Company series
by G. E. Stanley

Polly Berrien Berends
The Case of the Elevator Duck

Ann Cameron
Julian, Dream Doctor
Julian, Secret Agent
Julian's Glorious Summer

Adèle Geras
Little Swan

**Stephanie Spinner &
Jonathan Etra**
Aliens for Breakfast
Aliens for Lunch
Aliens for Dinner

Gloria Whelan
Next Spring an Oriole
Silver
Hannah
Night of the Full Moon
Shadow of the Wolf

Grades 3–5

FICTION
The Magic Elements Quartet
by Mallory Loehr
#1: Water Wishes
#2: Earth Magic
#3: Wind Spell
#4: Fire Dreams

Spider Kane Mysteries
by Mary Pope Osborne
#1: Spider Kane and the Mystery Under
the May-Apple
#2: Spider Kane and the Mystery at
Jumbo Nightcrawler's

NONFICTION
Thomas Conklin
The Titanic Sinks!

Elizabeth Cody Kimmel
Balto and the Great Race

Official Rules and Entry Information

I. NO PURCHASE NECESSARY. Print your name, address, phone number, date of birth, title of the book in which you saw this contest advertised, and a description of what you would take in your backpack on a Magic Tree House adventure (in 250 words or less) and mail to: MAGIC TREE HOUSE BACKPACK CONTEST, Random House Marketing Department, 1540 Broadway, 19th Floor, New York, NY 10036. Entries must be received by Random House no later than October 15, 2001. LIMIT ONE ENTRY PER PERSON. Random House will not be able to return your submission, so please keep a copy for your records.

II. ELIGIBILITY

The contest is open only to legal residents of the United States (excluding Puerto Rico and the state of Florida) who are between the ages 6 and 12 as of October 15, 2001. All federal, state, and local regulations apply. Void wherever prohibited or restricted by law. Employees of Random House, Inc., and of its parent, subsidiaries, and affiliates; members of their immediate families; and persons living in their households are not eligible to enter this contest. Random House is not responsible for lost, stolen, illegible, incomplete, or misdirected entries or those with postage due.

III. PRIZE

25 grand prize winners will each win a Magic Tree House backpack filled with Magic Tree House audiocassettes (approximate retail value $22.99 U.S. each). 1,500 first prize winners will each receive a Magic Tree House backpack (approximate retail value $4.99 U.S. each).

IV. WINNERS

Entries will be judged by the Random House Marketing Department on the basis of originality, style, and creativity. 25 grand prize winners and 1,500 first prize winners will be chosen on or around October 15, 2001, from all eligible entries received by the Random House Marketing Department within the entry deadline. Only the winners will be notified. The prizes will be awarded in the name of the winners' parents or legal guardians. Taxes, if any, are the winners' sole responsibility. The winners will be notified by mail on or around October 31, 2001. Winners' parents or legal guardians will be required to execute and return, within 14 days of receiving notification, affidavits of eligibility and release. Noncompliance within that period or the return of any notification as undeliverable will result in disqualification and the selection of an alternate winner. In the event of any other noncompliance with rules and conditions, the prize may be awarded to an alternate winner.

V. RESERVATIONS

Winners' parents or legal guardians, on winners' behalf, grant Random House the right to use and publish their legal names and states of residence online and in print, or any other media, in connection with the Contest. Acceptance of the prize constitutes permission for Random House to use winners' names and likenesses for editorials, advertising, and promotional purposes without payment of additional compensation unless prohibited by law. Other entry names will NOT be used for subsequent mail solicitation. For the names of the winners, available after October 31, 2001, please send a stamped, self-addressed envelope to: MAGIC TREE HOUSE BACKPACK WINNERS, Random House Marketing Department, 1540 Broadway, 19th Floor, New York, NY 10036. Washington and Vermont residents may omit return postage.

MARY POPE OSBORNE and WILL OSBORNE have been married for a number of years and live in New York City with their Norfolk terrier, Bailey. Mary is the author of over fifty books for children, and Will has worked for many years in the theater as an actor, director, and playwright. Together they have co-authored two books of Greek mythology.

Here's what Will and Mary have to say about working together on *Pirates:*

"Doing the research for *Pirates* was a lot of fun. Will visited the National Maritime Museum in Greenwich, England. Mary visited the Viking Ship Museum in Oslo, Norway. The most fun we had, though, was close to home. During Operation Sail 2000 in New York, we got to go on board a sailing ship that was built nearly 200 years ago! Our visit really brought the past alive and helped us understand a lot more about life at sea."